THIS JOURNAL BELONGS TO:

_____

I started writing on:

this day _____

in the year _____

in the city of _____

and I was _____ *years old.*

I filled up the last page on:

this day _____

in the year _____

in the city of _____

and I was _____ *years old.*

It was given to me by:

_____

SECOND EDITION

MY NATURE BOOK

A JOURNAL AND ACTIVITY BOOK FOR KIDS

LINDA KRANZ

TAYLOR TRADE PUBLISHING
Lanham • New York • Boulder • Toronto • Plymouth, UK

Designed by Lois A. Rainwater
Illustrations by Linda Garrow and John F. McGee
Digital illustrations composed by Lois A. Rainwater

Published by Taylor Trade Publishing
An imprint of The Rowman & Littlefield Publishing Group, Inc.
4501 Forbes Boulevard, Suite 200, Lanham, Maryland 20706
www.rowman.com

10 Thornbury Road, Plymouth PL6 7PP, United Kingdom

Distributed by National Book Network

British Library Cataloguing in Publication Information Available

Library of Congress Cataloging-in-Publication Information
Kranz, Linda, 1955–
My nature book : a journal and activity book for kids / Linda Kranz. — Second edition.
pages cm
Audience: 6+
Audience: K to grade 3.
ISBN 978-1-58979-822-9 (pbk. : alk. paper) 1. Nature—Miscellanea—Juvenile literature.
2. Diaries—Juvenile literature. I. Title.
QH81.K823 2013
508—dc23
2013008105

∞™ The paper used in this publication meets the minimum requirements of
American National Standard for Information Sciences—
Permanence of Paper for Printed Library Materials, ANSI/NISO Z39.48-1992.

Printed in Selangor Darul Ehsan Malaysia July 2023

A thank-you to those who had the foresight
to set aside land for national parks,

national monuments, state parks, city parks,
and wilderness areas so that all of us
can enjoy our time outdoors.

—L.K.

A NOTE
FROM THE AUTHOR

We have seen black bears, foxes, horned toads, raccoons, snakes, skunks, lizards, deer, coyotes, elk, tarantulas, and rabbits. Each encounter has its own story. We have captured some on film, but most sightings I have only written about in my journals.

Here's a journal entry I wrote several years ago as we were about to head back home after our annual trip to the mountains:

"

The cabin was cozy. Four windows with curtains that tied back in the day and fell shut for privacy at night. A comfortable place where we could kick back and relax. Mostly it was a dry place to sleep because late in the summer we always seem to encounter daily afternoon or nighttime thunderstorms. We spent our days out in the forest by rivers and streams, watching clouds build above the pine-covered canyons. Reading, fishing, carving wood to float tiny boats downstream, skipping rocks across the calm part of the river, watching butterflies, searching for four-leafed clovers, or drawing the landscape around us.

Then before we'd know it, the days would be almost over. We always planned it so that we would have a good vantage point to watch the colorful sunset and then we would head back as the stars were coming out. In the evening, the cabin was a place where conversations were plentiful and laughter filled the small spaces inside. After dinner there were board games and stories.

During the night, thunderstorms would often sneak into the valley and the metal roof on the cabin really had a way of accentuating the sound of the rain pouring down. A few times we couldn't even hear ourselves talk it was so

Our family was out hiking one weekend not long ago when we spotted a mother hummingbird and her tiny nest—what a rare sight! We watched her sitting there silent and motionless. Not wanting to disturb her, we continued on our trek upstream. That afternoon we also saw a very long, sleek gopher snake; a tall great blue heron; and a turtle sunning himself on a fallen branch in the creek. Sometimes when we're out hiking, we don't see a single animal. Then there are days like this that are exciting and fun to talk about with family and friends.

loud. *We would watch the electric show out our windows and feel the ground shake beneath us. Soon, the storm moved on and we were able to fall asleep so we would* be rested for another day outdoors.**"**

I love rereading the adventures we've had over the years as we explored different places. I'm glad we have the journals and photographs to remind us of these very special times.

And now you can capture your memories from nature inside this journal!

TIPS FOR JOURNAL WRITERS

This is your journal—a place for you to write about and illustrate the experiences that are uniquely your own. We all view the world in our own ways. Journaling is sometimes even better than photographs for helping us to remember a time or place because we can describe not only the sights, but also the sounds and smells, and most importantly, how we were feeling at the time. Someday you may want to go back to your journal, and the more descriptive your entries are, the more they will help you remember those days gone by.

Always date your pages and write in the day of the week. Journaling captures a time that will never be the same again.

You will notice that I have included lots of "thought starters" to get your ideas flowing. There are also many blank pages where you can write down your own experiences, or draw anything you want. This journal can easily slip into your backpack so that you can write notes or draw pictures while you are relaxing on the hiking trail. Or you can write or draw on the ride back, or perhaps you will want to wait until you are at home in your own room just before bedtime. Whichever you choose, be sure to set aside time to record your thoughts while your memory is still fresh, and these pages will fill up easily.

So, what are you waiting for? Grab your journal and go out and explore!

—LINDA KRANZ

Find a comfortable spot.
Listen for the sounds all around you.

_____ What do you hear?

_____ How does the air smell?

_____ What is the temperature like?

_____ Close your eyes and sit very still.

_____ When you are ready

_____ open your eyes and write about

_____ what you discover.

_____ Continue to sit very still.

_____ Notice the movement around you.

_____ What do you see?

_____ Write about what you discover.

_____

_____

_____

_____

_____

If you could
invent something
that would be
very useful
or that would
be beneficial
to someone
who spends a
lot of time
outdoors, what
would it be?
Describe it here.

TRAVEL NOTES!

DATE: _____   DAY OF THE WEEK: _____

THE COST OF GAS: _____   TIME WE LEFT: _____   WHEN WE RETURNED: _____

TODAY WE DROVE TO: _____

_____

WHY WE WANTED TO VISIT THIS PLACE: / HOW WE HEARD ABOUT IT: _____

_____

WE'VE BEEN HERE BEFORE: / THIS IS OUR FIRST TIME HERE: _____

_____

WHAT THE WEATHER WAS LIKE: _____

_____

INTERESTING THINGS THAT WE SAW: _____

_____

HOW WE SPENT THE DAY: _____

_____

NEXT TIME WE GO BACK TO THIS PLACE, I WANT TO: _____

_____

WHAT I WILL REMEMBER MOST ABOUT THIS DAY: _____

_____

_____

_____

Write about something you discovered that you never noticed before.

_____

_____

_____

_____

_____

_____

_____

_____

_____

_____

_____

_____

_____

_____

_____

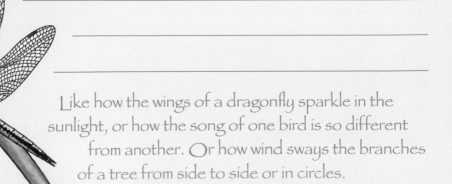

Like how the wings of a dragonfly sparkle in the sunlight, or how the song of one bird is so different from another. Or how wind sways the branches of a tree from side to side or in circles.

Ask your family what they like most about being in nature. They might teach you something that you've never thought about.

DRAW whatever you want on these pages.

BELIEVED TO BE RELATED TO THEIR NATURAL HABIT OF FINDING FOOD IN WATER.

"WASH" EVERYTHING THEY EAT, BUT THIS BEHAVIOR IS NOT RELATED TO CLEANLINESS. IT'S

Let your imagination go WILD! • SLEEPING BIRDS DO NOT FALL OFF BRANCHES BECAUSE THEY HAVE A WAY OF "LOCKING" THEIR FEET AROUND A PERCH. THERE IS A TENDON IN THE BIRDS' FEET THAT AUTOMATICALLY LOCKS THEM IN PLACE • ACCORDING TO POPULAR MYTH, RACCOONS

What types of weather extremes have you experienced?

_____

_____

The hottest

temperature? _____

_____

The coldest? _____

_____

The most rain? _____

_____

The most snow? _____

_____

A hail-storm? _____

_____

The driest summer? _____

_____

A drought? _____

_____

Lightning that was _____

too close for _____

comfort? _____

Thundersnow?

A hurricane?

A tornado?

Describe your experiences.

Now that you had this experience, what advice would you give to others who are about to find themselves in extreme weather?

A FUN PROJECT FOR YOU!

Make Banana Bread or Muffins to Take with You on Hiking Trips
This is a great snack to eat on your hike, or on the ride home.

Ingredients:

- ❖ 2¼ cups (315 g) sifted flour
- ❖ ¾ tsp (2.75 g/3.7 ml) baking soda
- ❖ ⅛ tsp (.75 g/.6 ml) salt
- ❖ ¼ cup (½ stick/55 g) butter, at room temperature
- ❖ ¾ cup (150 g) sugar
- ❖ 2 eggs
- ❖ 2 medium-size ripe bananas, mashed (about ¾ cup/1.8 dl)
- ❖ ½ cup (1.2 dl/115 g) sour cream

Optional (choose one):

- ❖ ½ cup (55 g) chopped walnuts or pecans, or
- ❖ ½ cup (60 g) dried cranberries, or
- ❖ ½ cup (85 g) chocolate chips

Preheat the oven to 350° (175°C). Butter and flour a large loaf pan or muffin tin, or spray with cooking oil. Sift together flour, baking soda, and salt. In a large bowl, cream butter and sugar until light and fluffy. Beat in eggs. Add sifted dry ingredients, alternating with banana and sour cream. Mix until just blended. Blend in nuts, cranberries, or chocolate chips, if using, and pour into loaf pan or muffin tin. Bake loaf 1 hour or muffins for 25 minutes, or until toothpick inserted in center comes out clean. Remove from oven and let cool on rack. Slice loaf and wrap in plastic wrap or place in a resealable bag. Freeze. The bread will be ready for your next outing. If you don't have a cooler, you can take the frozen slices with you and by the time you're ready to eat the bread, it will be thawed. You could also freeze the muffins to take with you (wrap them individually in plastic wrap).

ABOUT MY PROJECT!

HOW DID MY BANANA BREAD TASTE?

DID OTHER PEOPLE ENJOY IT?

WILL I MAKE IT AGAIN? IF SO, WOULD I CHANGE ANYTHING ABOUT THE RECIPE?

 **DRAW** Do you remember the brightest

Draw it, or put a photo here.

rainbow you have ever seen?

DRAW

WHAT MAKES A RAINBOW? WHEN IT RAINS, RAINDROPS FILL THE AIR. THE RAINDROPS ACT AS PRISMS. IF SUNLIGHT FILTERS THROUGH THE RAINDROPS AT JUST THE RIGHT ANGLE, A RAINBOW WILL APPEAR. NOTICE—TO SEE A RAINBOW THE SUN MUST BE BEHIND YOU.

Do you think there are animals out there in the world that have never been seen by a human?

_____

_____

_____

If so, what _____

do you _____

think they _____

look like? _____

And what _____

would you _____

name them? _____

_____

_____

_____

_____

_____

_____

_____

Draw what you think those animals would look like.

Do they look like the names you gave them?

Ask your parents, a relative, a teacher, or a friend how areas around your town have changed over the years since they have lived there.

_____

_____

_____

_____

_____

_____

_____

_____

_____

_____

_____

_____

_____

_____

_____

_____

How are things the same? _____

Write down some historical facts _____

and other interesting things that you learn. _____

You could learn

more about how

your town has

changed by

going to a museum,

a national park

or monument,

an arboretum,

or visiting your

chamber of commerce.

 **DRAW**

On a nice day when there are plenty of puffy white clouds in the sky,

DRAW

Lie on your back in a patch of green grass. Make shapes out of the clouds. Draw some of the shapes you see.

A FUN PROJECT FOR YOU!

Make Luminarias
[loo-muh-NAR-ee-uhs]

You will need:

- ❖ medium to large clean and dry empty metal soup can or coffee can (try to find a can that is smooth on the sides)
- ❖ hammer
- ❖ nail
- ❖ small votive candle
- ❖ permanent marker

Draw a design on the outside of your can using the permanent marker. A star, a tree, a snowman, letters or numbers, or any shape you want. (You could also draw the pattern on paper first, cut it out, and trace around it onto the can.) Fill the can with water. Freeze it. Make sure it is frozen solid when you begin your project.

Lay the frozen can on a thick towel to help stabilize it, and to give you a better working surface. With the help of an adult, use the nail to hammer holes along the lines of your design. Pound the holes all the way through the sides of the can. Find a place to leave your can while the ice melts, or set the can in warm water to melt the ice more quickly. When the ice has melted, dry your can completely. Be careful! The edges of the holes inside the can will be very sharp. Carefully place the candle inside. Put your candle outside where it can be seen by passers-by. Wait for sunset and ask an adult to light the candle for you. You could make several luminarias and they could light the way to your front door!

ABOUT MY PROJECT!

WHAT SHAPES DID I DESIGN FOR MY CANS?

DID MY NEIGHBORS TELL ME HOW BEAUTIFUL THEY WERE?

WILL I MAKE IT AGAIN? IF SO, WHAT WILL I DO DIFFERENTLY?

DRAW If you could draw the wind,
what would it look like?

Are you a good traveler?

Why or why not?

What do you like or dislike

about waking up in a new place?

If you could spend
a week anywhere that
you choose, where
would it be and what
would you like to do there?

TRAVEL NOTES!

DATE: _____ DAY OF THE WEEK: _____

THE COST OF GAS: _____ TIME WE LEFT: _____ WHEN WE RETURNED: _____

TODAY WE DROVE TO: _____
_____

WHY WE WANTED TO VISIT THIS PLACE: / HOW WE HEARD ABOUT IT: _____
_____

WE'VE BEEN HERE BEFORE: / THIS IS OUR FIRST TIME HERE: _____
_____

WHAT THE WEATHER WAS LIKE: _____
_____

INTERESTING THINGS THAT WE SAW: _____
_____

HOW WE SPENT THE DAY: _____
_____

NEXT TIME WE GO BACK TO THIS PLACE, I WANT TO: _____
_____

WHAT I WILL REMEMBER MOST ABOUT THIS DAY: _____
_____
_____
_____

What would you like to learn more about when it comes to the subject of nature?

 **DRAW** or paste your photos on these pages.

"THE EARTH LAUGHS IN FLOWERS." —RALPH WALDO EMERSON • "THE SMELL OF RAIN IS RICH WITH LIFE." —ESTELA PORTILLO TRAMBLEY • "TEACHING CHILDREN ABOUT THE NATURAL WORLD SHCULD BE TREATED AS ONE OF THE MOST IMPORTANT EVENTS IN THEIR LIVES." —THOMAS BERRY • "KEEP SOME SOUVENIRS OF YOUR PAST,

A FUN PROJECT FOR YOU!

Take a Nature Walk

Take a walk around your neighborhood. Write about what you see. Check off any animals, insects, or reptiles that you might have seen along the way:

SNAKE ☐

FROG ☐

CHIPMUNK ☐

LADYBUG ☐

LIZARD ☐   SQUIRREL ☐   _____ ☐

SKUNK ☐   SPIDER ☐   _____ ☐

ARMADILLO ☐   CRICKET ☐   _____ ☐

DRAGONFLY ☐   BIRD ☐   _____ ☐

ABOUT MY PROJECT!

WHERE DID I GO ON MY NATURE WALK?

HOW MANY ITEMS DID I CHECK OFF THE LIST?

WHERE WOULD I LIKE TO GO NEXT TIME?

Good times are for remembering.
    Write about good times you've had in nature
that you will NEVER forget.

_____

_____

_____

_____

_____

_____

_____

_____

_____

_____

_____

_____

_____

_____

_____

_____

_____

_____

_____

National parks, national monuments, and state parks are treasures.

They offer facts and history of a particular area. They have knowledgeable experts and volunteers that can answer your questions. They have established hiking trails and open spaces for you to enjoy.

Which parks have
you visited?
What did you find
most interesting?
Do you have
suggestions
that you think
would make the
park experience
more interesting
to you and your
family and
other visitors?

SQUIRREL,

COYOTE,

DEER . . .

have you ever

thought about the

names of animals?

They were named

long ago.

If you could

rename them,

what would you

call them?

Or, would you leave

them as they are?

Do any of these sights and sounds remind you of a place or time?

The sound of a
cricket chirping?

_____
_____
_____

The sound of waves
lapping against
the shore?

_____
_____
_____
_____

The feel of warm sand
between your toes?

_____
_____
_____

The rumbling of
thunder off in the
distance?

_____
_____
_____
_____

Flashes of lightning
in the sky?

_____
_____

Leaves changing as the
termperature cools?

_____
_____

Watching the
full moon rise?

The sound of fresh
snow crunching
under your feet?

A campfire crackling?

The refreshing smell
in the air after
a rain shower?

New buds on the trees
as springtime arrives?

A sunrise and
the soft colors
in the clouds?

A FUN PROJECT FOR YOU!

Trail-Ready Peanut Butter Cookies
(GF—Gluten Free)

Ingredients:

- ❖ 1 cup peanut butter (smooth or chunky)
- ❖ ¾ cup white sugar, plus extra for sprinkling
- ❖ ⅓ cup lightly packed brown sugar, plus extra for sprinkling
- ❖ 1 egg
- ❖ ½ tsp vanilla

Preheat the oven to 350° and line two baking sheets with parchment paper. In a medium bowl, mix all ingredients with a rubber spatula or spoon until well combined. Using your hands, roll a heaping tablespoon of dough into a ball and place on the baking sheet. Repeat with remaining dough, leaving space for cookies to spread. With a soft touch, use a fork to push a criss-cross pattern on top of each cookie. Do not flatten all the way. Sprinkle the top of each cookie with a pinch of each type of sugar. Bake for about 12 minutes. The cookies will still feel extremely soft to the touch. After removing from oven, allow the cookies to cool for at least 20 minutes before handling them. They will become firm as they cool. Store in an air-tight container and freeze. Take out just before you leave home and bring these treats to enjoy a delicious snack on the trail. Everyone will love these treats!

ABOUT MY PROJECT!

HOW DID MY TRAIL-READY PEANUT BUTTER COOKIES TASTE?

DID OTHER PEOPLE ENJOY THEM?

WILL I MAKE THEM AGAIN? IF SO, WOULD I CHANGE ANYTHING ABOUT THE RECIPE?

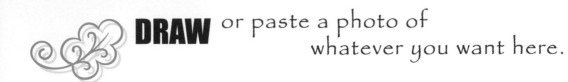 **DRAW** or paste a photo of whatever you want here.

ANIMAL SIGHTINGS!
WHERE WERE YOU?
WHAT ANIMALS DID YOU SEE THERE?

DATE: _____ PLACE: _____

THE ANIMALS I SAW: _____

_____

_____

_____

_____

_____

DATE: _____ PLACE: _____

THE ANIMALS I SAW: _____

_____

_____

_____

_____

DATE: _____ PLACE: _____

THE ANIMALS I SAW: _____

_____

_____

_____

Explore places around your neighborhood.
Be a tourist in your own town.

Often, beautiful places are overlooked close to home. Look on a map for new places to discover with your family. Write about what you discover.

What is the most amazing sight that you've seen on your travels?

A mountain range?

A waterfall?

A vast desert?

An interesting animal?

What made it so striking?

 **DRAW** "I AM WELL AGAIN, I CAME TO LIFE IN THE COOL WINDS AND CRYSTAL

TWICE? IT IS A MYTH. THE EMPIRE STATE BUILDING IN NEW YORK CITY IS STRUCK 20 TO 30 TIMES EACH YEAR.

HENRY DAVID THOREAU • HAVE YOU EVER HEARD THAT LIGHTNING NEVER STRIKES THE SAME PLACE

WATERS OF THE MOUNTAINS . . . " —JOHN MUIR • "EACH NEW YEAR IS A SURPRISE TO US. WE FIND THAT WE HAD VIRTUALLY FORGOTTEN THE NOTE OF EACH BIRD, AND WHEN WE HEAR IT AGAIN, IT IS REMEMBERED LIKE A DREAM, REMINDING US OF A PREVIOUS STATE OF EXISTENCE . . . THE VOICE OF NATURE IS ALWAYS ENCOURAGING." —

If you were given
a canoe, camping gear,
and food for a week,
and you could choose
one person to go
along with you on
the trip, who would
you choose to go with
you and where would
you go? What do you
think your adventure
would be like? Describe
your dream getaway.

Camouflage is a natural way for animals, reptiles, and insects to blend in with their surroundings. Have you ever been surprised by an insect or animal when you have been out exploring? Be aware next time and write down a few of the things you discovered.

DRAW

"I AM INCLINED TO THINK THAT THE FLOWERS WE MOST LOVE

ARE THOSE WE KNEW WHEN WE WERE VERY YOUNG." —DOROTHY THOMPSON • "HE THAT

PLANTS A TREE LOVES OTHERS BESIDES HIMSELF." —THOMAS FULLER • "I NEVER BEFORE KNEW THE FULL VALUE OF TREES. UNDER

THEM I BREAKFAST, DINE, WRITE, READ AND RECEIVE MY COMPANY." —THOMAS JEFFERSON

A FUN PROJECT FOR YOU!

Chewy Oatmeal Raisin Cookies
(GF—Gluten Free)

Ingredients:

- ❖ 2 sticks of butter (1 cup)
- ❖ 1½ cups packed brown sugar
- ❖ 2 eggs
- ❖ 1 tsp vanilla
- ❖ 1½ cups gluten-free flour mix (if your mix doesn't include xanthan gum, try using ¾ tsp xanthan gum
- ❖ 1 tsp baking soda
- ❖ 1 tsp pumpkin pie spice or cinnamon
- ❖ ½ tsp salt (optional but not needed if your flour mix has salt added)
- ❖ 3 cups certified gluten-free rolled oats
- ❖ 1 cup raisins

Optional:

- ❖ 1½ cups butterscotch chips or chocolate chips

Preheat the oven to 350°. Line cookie sheets with parchment paper or use a non-stick spray. In the bowl of your mixer, cream butter and brown sugar. Add eggs and vanilla, and beat. Add the gluten-free flour mix (and xanthan gum, if needed), baking soda, pumpkin pie spice or cinnamon, and salt, if desired. Mix until well-blended. Add the oats and mix. Add the raisins (or omit raisins and add chocolate or butterscotch chips, if desired). For added variety you can also split the batter into two separate bowls and add chocolate chips or butter-scotch chips in one half and raisins in the other half. Scoop teaspoon- or tablespoon-sized bits of dough onto the cookie sheet. Leave room for spreading as the cookies bake. Bake for 10 to 14 minutes or until the edges are golden brown and the centers appear set. Allow the cookies to cool on the baking sheet for about 5–10 minutes before removing to a rack to finish cooling. When cooled, store cookies in an air-tight container in the freezer. Take out cookies when you are heading off for a hike. Enjoy on the trail.

ABOUT MY PROJECT!

HOW DID MY CHEWY OATMEAL RAISIN COOKIES TASTE?

DID OTHER PEOPLE ENJOY THEM?

WILL I MAKE THEM AGAIN? IF SO, WOULD I CHANGE ANYTHING ABOUT THE RECIPE?

What are the ten things you enjoy about nature? Keep adding to this list.

1

2

3

4

5

6

7

8

9

10

DRAW

Fireflies, or lightning bugs, are found throughout the tropical and temperate regions of the world. In the United States they live mostly east of the Mississippi River. One reason fireflies glow is to attract mates. Another reason is to avoid predators. Fireflies are filled with a nasty-tasting chemical called lucibufagins that predators don't like. Yet that doesn't stop some predators from eating them. Frogs have been known to devour large numbers of fireflies until they also begin to glow. Draw your own fireflies on this page.

Write more thoughts on this page.

Finish one of these thought starters...

Today I discovered . . . or, In a perfect world . . .

Finish one of these thought starters...

What if . . . or, When I think about this, I can't help but smile . . .

S
P
R
I
N
G

Find a tree in your yard, your neighborhood, or at your. . . . . . .

tree as the seasons change. . . . . . .

S
U
M
M
E
R

F
A
L
L

. . . . . school that you can watch for a year. Pay attention to the

. . . . . Draw how the tree looks each season.

W
I
N
T
E
R

**How does the night sky
in your town or city compare to the sky
in the wilderness?**

_____

_____

_____

_____

_____

_____

_____

_____

_____

_____

_____

_____

_____

_____

_____

_____

_____

_____

_____

_____

_____

_____

Write about a few of the "firsts" in your life.

The first time
you caught
a fish.

_____

_____

_____

_____

_____

The first time
you saw a
wild animal
in nature.

_____

_____

_____

_____

_____

_____

The first time
you went hiking.

_____

_____

_____

_____

The first time
you swam
in a lake.

_____

_____

_____

_____

_____

_____

_____

_____

_____

_____

_____

_____

_____

_____

_____

_____

_____

_____

The first time
you climbed
a tree.

The first time
you noticed wild
animal tracks
when you were
out on a hike.

The first time
you saw a falling
star.

The first time
you crossed
a creek by
jumping from
rock to rock.

If you could write your own rules about the natural world, what would they be? Why would your rules be helpful and important?

_____

_____

_____

_____

_____

_____

_____

_____

_____

_____

_____

_____

_____

_____

When you are out hiking or camping, pack out everything that you pack in.

When you are hiking or camping, be sure to bring a small trash bag with you so you can leave the natural place that you visit just as you found it. Did you know that certain items take a long time to biodegrade? For instance:

Paper	2–5 months
Orange peels	6 months
Plastic bags	10–20 years
Tin cans	50–100 years
Aluminum cans	80–100 years
Glass bottles	1 million years
Plastic bottles	Never

Write whatever you want on this page.

Let your imagination SOAR!

Have you ever seen something that made you sad when you were out exploring?

What was it?

_____

_____

_____

_____

_____

_____

_____

Did you talk about it with

your parents or an adult?

_____

_____

_____

_____

_____

_____

_____

_____

_____

True-life nature survival stories that you've read or heard about.

Write about five beautiful things that you noticed today.

Date:

1.

2.

3.

4.

5.

Date:

1.

2.

3.

4.

5.

Date:

1.

2.

3.

4.

5.

ANIMAL SIGHTINGS!
WHERE WERE YOU?
WHAT ANIMALS DID YOU SEE THERE?

DATE: _____ PLACE: _____

THE ANIMALS I SAW: _____

_____

_____

_____

_____

_____

DATE: _____ PLACE: _____

THE ANIMALS I SAW: _____

_____

_____

_____

_____

_____

DATE: _____ PLACE: _____

THE ANIMALS I SAW: _____

_____

_____

_____

DRAW

Butterflies go through four stages of life. An adult butterfly lays an egg. The egg hatches into a caterpillar larva. The caterpillar forms the chrysalis. The chrysalis matures into a butterfly.

Fill up these pages with inspiring quotes, helpful sayings, and words from writers you admire.

_____

_____

_____

_____

_____

_____

_____

_____

_____

_____

_____

_____

_____

Thirty days hath September,
April, June, and November.
All the rest have thirty-one,
Excepting February alone,
And that has twenty-eight days clear,
And twenty-nine in each leap year.
—Mother Goose

"If we want children to flourish, to become truly empowered, then let us allow them to love the earth before we ask them to save it. Perhaps this is what Thoreau had in mind when he said, 'the more slowly trees grow at first, the sounder they are at the core, and I think the same is true of human beings.'"
—David Sobel

Have you ever traveled a scenic byway road? A scenic trail? What do you remember about the drive? Are there other roads that you would like to travel on someday?

TRAVEL NOTES!

DATE: _____ DAY OF THE WEEK: _____

THE COST OF GAS: _____ TIME WE LEFT: _____ WHEN WE RETURNED: _____

TODAY WE DROVE TO: _____

_____

WHY WE WANTED TO VISIT THIS PLACE: / HOW WE HEARD ABOUT IT:

_____

WE'VE BEEN HERE BEFORE: / THIS IS OUR FIRST TIME HERE:

_____

WHAT THE WEATHER WAS LIKE:

_____

INTERESTING THINGS THAT WE SAW:

_____

HOW WE SPENT THE DAY:

_____

NEXT TIME WE GO BACK TO THIS PLACE, I WANT TO:

_____

WHAT I WILL REMEMBER MOST ABOUT THIS DAY:

_____

_____

_____

Write more thoughts on this page.

Write about a few nature books
you have read that have held your interest.

What did you like best about them?

_____

_____

_____

_____

_____

_____

What did you learn when you read them?

_____

_____

_____

_____

_____

_____

Perhaps one day you could become an expert on a subject
and write your own book.

DRAW

Look for unusual or surprising things in nature the next time you are out hiking—like a tree root curled around a rock or a cactus pad shaped like a heart.

DRAW

Draw some of those unique things here. Add to these sketches over time as you find more unique things. Remember to date your drawings.

How would you describe the forest, the desert, the prairie, the ocean, or any of your favorite landscapes to someone who has never seen them?

If you want to learn more about different places, go to the library, or check it out on the Internet.

Write whatever you want here.

If you could talk to someone in another country about the kinds of wildlife there, who would you want to talk to? What would you ask them?

_____

_____

_____

_____

_____

_____

_____

_____

_____

_____

_____

_____

_____

_____

Which explorers do you admire?

Lewis and Clark discovered a route to the West Coast.

John Wesley Powell mapped the Colorado River.

If you could be written about in history books for something you did, what would you want to be known for?

What do you think it would be like to be the very first person to discover a place?

**If you could go back in time or go into the future,
where would you go and what would you want to learn?**

DRAW

Draw the most beautiful sunset you have ever seen.

At the bottom of the page, write the date and place where you saw it.

Do you have a favorite place in nature where you like to go?

Why do you like it so much?

_____

_____

_____

_____

How long does it take you to get there?

_____

_____

What do you like to do there?

_____

_____

_____

_____

Describe what the area looks like.

_____

_____

_____

_____

Has something someone said or something you read made an impression on how you view the natural world?

Perhaps a guest speaker at school?

_____

_____

_____

_____

_____

_____

A show on television?

_____

_____

_____

_____

_____

_____

An article in a magazine?

Or a book that you read?

A FUN PROJECT FOR YOU!

Make Delicious
Energy-Boosting Trail Mix

Ingredients:

In a large bowl mix ⅓ cup (80 ml) each
of the following ingredients:

- ❖ dried cranberries
- ❖ raisins
- ❖ stick or mini pretzels
- ❖ Multi-bran Chex cereal
- ❖ Cheerios cereal
- ❖ sunflower seeds
- ❖ unsalted nuts
  (peanuts, pecans, almonds, cashews, etc.)
- ❖ dried banana chips
- ❖ If it's not too hot outside, you could also add
  mini chocolate chips or M&M's

Store your trail mix in a resealable plastic bag, or in an air-tight container.

ABOUT MY PROJECT!

WAS MY TRAIL MIX TASTY?

DID OTHER PEOPLE ENJOY IT?

WILL I MAKE IT AGAIN? IF SO, WOULD I CHANGE ANYTHING ABOUT THE RECIPE?

DRAW

SAY THE WAY THERE SEEMS LONGER THAN THE WAY BACK. DO YOU THINK THIS IS TRUE?

NOTICE CERTAIN LANDMARKS AS YOU PASS THEM SO YOU CAN FIND YOUR WAY BACK EASILY. • SOME

GROUP WHILE HIKING, STAY PUT. CARRY A WHISTLE. BLOW IT FROM TIME TO TIME. REMEMBER TO STAY PUT. BE ALERT. • IF YOU GET BITTEN OR STUNG BY A SNAKE, BEE, OR OTHER INSECT OR ANIMAL, STAY CALM. TELL AN ADULT. SEEK IMMEDIATE MEDICAL ATTENTION. • PAY ATTENTION WHEN YOU ARE HIKING. FOLLOW THE PATH.

TRAVEL NOTES!

DATE: _____ DAY OF THE WEEK: _____

THE COST OF GAS: _____ TIME WE LEFT: _____ WHEN WE RETURNED: _____

TODAY WE DROVE TO: _____
_____

WHY WE WANTED TO VISIT THIS PLACE: / HOW WE HEARD ABOUT IT:
_____

WE'VE BEEN HERE BEFORE: / THIS IS OUR FIRST TIME HERE:
_____

WHAT THE WEATHER WAS LIKE:
_____

INTERESTING THINGS THAT WE SAW:
_____

HOW WE SPENT THE DAY:
_____

NEXT TIME WE GO BACK TO THIS PLACE, I WANT TO:
_____

WHAT I WILL REMEMBER MOST ABOUT THIS DAY:
_____
_____
_____

Ladybugs or lady beetles are a very beneficial group of insects. A single ladybug may consume as many as 5,000 aphids in its lifetime. Aphids are tiny insects that suck the juices from plants, weakening their leaves and stems.

DRAW

WHEN YOU ARE OUT FOR A WALK, FIND LEAVES OF DIFFERENT SIZES

LEAF COLORS. SUNNY AUTUMN DAYS ARE NEEDED FOR THE BRIGHTEST COLOR DISPLAYS.

LEAVES. WHEN DAYS ARE SHORTER AND THE SUNLIGHT LEVELS DROP, THIS ALSO PLAYS A ROLE IN FALL

AND SHAPES. TRACE AROUND THEM. NOTICE THEIR DETAILS. USE COLORED PENCILS TO SHOW THE VARIETY OF COLORS YOU HAVE FOUND. OR PASTE PHOTOS OF BEAUTIFUL LEAVES THAT YOU HAVE SEEN ON THESE PAGES. • AS WARM SUMMER DAYS FADE AND COOLER TEMPERATURES SET IN, A CHEMICAL REACTION IS TRIGGERED IN

Make a Water Window to Look in a Creek, Stream, River, or Lake

You Will Need:

- ❖ large metal can
- ❖ large clear plastic bag
- ❖ large rubber band

Remove the top and bottom of the metal can. Place the plastic bag over one end of the can. Secure the bag with a large rubber band. Trim bag if necessary. Place the plastic bag-covered end of the can in the water and look through the open end. Now you can see down into the water!

Or, you can also make the water window using the following instead:

- ❖ ½ gallon (2L) cardboard milk carton
- ❖ heavy plastic wrap
- ❖ large rubber band
- ❖ masking tape or electrical tape

Cut the top and bottom off the carton. Wrap plastic wrap up and over the sides of one end. Tape plastic wrap securely. Place rubber band on the bottom half of the carton to keep the wrap tight and secure.

ABOUT MY PROJECT!

HOW DID MY WATER WINDOW TURN OUT?

_____

_____

_____

_____

_____

WHAT DID I LEARN?

_____

_____

_____

_____

_____

WILL I MAKE ANOTHER ONE? IF SO, WHAT WILL I DO DIFFERENTLY?

_____

_____

_____

_____

_____

Has the weather ever caused you to change your plans? When? How did it turn out? Describe the worst thing about it and the best thing about it.

 **DRAW**

Star watching
is fun. Take time
to look up at the
night sky. Can
you find any
constellations?
If you watch
long enough,
you might even
see a falling star.
Draw a picture
of a falling star
or constellation.

DRAW

It is estimated
that there are
20,000 different
species of ants.
For this reason,
ants have been
called Earth's
most successful
species. They can
be found
almost anywhere
on the planet.

Pay attention to the sounds you hear as you wake up each morning.

How early do
you hear the
birds start to
sing? What other
sounds do you
hear as you lie
still and listen?

Have you ever been camping or been to a summer camp?

What was it like?
If you haven't, would you
like to try camping
sometime? What do you
think it would be like?

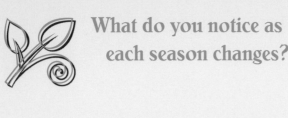

What do you notice as each season changes?

_____

_____

_____

_____

_____

_____

_____

What is your   _____

favorite season   _____

of the year?   _____

Why?

_____

_____

_____

_____

_____

What's the weather like on your birthday? How does it change from year to year?

DRAW

BEAUTY IF WE ONLY HAVE THE EYES TO SEE THEM."—JOHN RUSKIN • "I GO TO NATURE TO BE SOOTHED AND HEALED, AND TO HAVE MY SENSES PUT IN TUNE ONCE MORE."—JOHN BURROUGHS • "FEW FORMS OF LIFE ARE SO ENGAGING AS BIRDS."—ELLEN GLASGOW • "TRAVEL AND CHANGE OF PLACE IMPART NEW VIGOR TO THE MIND."

 Write whatever you want on this page.
Let your imagination go WILD!

TRAVEL CHECKLIST

WHERE ARE WE GOING?

WATER BOTTLE ☐   SUNSCREEN ☐   INSECT REPELLENT ☐

FIRST-AID KIT ☐   HAT ☐   COMFORTABLE SHOES ☐

RAIN GEAR ☐   THERMOS ☐   SNACKS ☐

BINOCULARS ☐   CAMERA ☐ EXTRA FILM (MEMORY CARD) ☐

LIGHT JACKET ☐   TRASH BAG ☐   NOTEBOOK/PENCILS ☐

WHISTLE ☐ MAGNIFYING GLASS ☐   FLASHLIGHT/BATTERIES ☐

ADD YOUR OWN LIST OF THINGS YOU MIGHT NEED:

 **DRAW**

There are
750 kinds of
trees in North
America.
The trees that
lose their leaves
are called
deciduous.
Evergreens keep
their leaves
year-round.
Draw your
favorite type of
tree, or place a
photo here.

Sometimes a song will bring back a memory. When you hear a certain song on the radio, does it remind you of a special place that you have visited?

Name a few songs.

_____

_____

_____

_____

_____

Write about the memories these songs bring back when you hear them.

_____

_____

_____

_____

_____

_____

_____

_____

Look back through this journal and write about what you feel when you read your entries and look at your drawings. What makes your finished journal special?

_____
_____
_____
_____
_____
_____
_____
_____
_____
_____
_____
_____
_____
_____
_____
_____
_____
_____

LINDA KRANZ is the author of eight journals, a craft book, *Let's Rock! Rock Painting for Kids,* and three other books: *Only One You, You Be You,* and *Love You When . . .*

Linda would love to hear about one of your favorite, true-life adventure, wildlife, camping, or getaway stories, or to hear how you are enjoying your *My Nature Book: A Journal and Activity Book for Kids.*

You can write to her at:

Linda Kranz

P.O. Box 2404

Flagstaff, AZ 86003-2404

Also, find out more about Linda on her website: www.lindakranz.com.

Links to research:

www.nps.gov

www.americasstateparks.org

www.byways.org